Seasons
Scrapbook

Written by Charlotte Raby
Illustrated by Christine Jenny

Park

We'll find lots of things in the park.

We'll find flowers.

We'll find bees.

7

We'll find leaves.

9

We'll find a robin.

10

Park

We found lots of things in the park.

Seasons

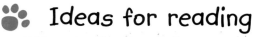

Ideas for reading

Written by Clare Dowdall BA(Ed), MA(Ed)
Lecturer and Primary Literacy Consultant

Learning objectives: read simple words by sounding out and blending the phonemes all through the word from left to right; show an understanding of how information can be found in non-fiction texts to answer questions about where, who, why and how; use talk to organise, sequence and clarify thinking, ideas, feelings and events; use language to imagine and recreate roles and experiences; extend their vocabulary, exploring the meanings and sounds of new words

Curriculum links: Knowledge and Understanding of the World: Exploration and investigation; Place

High frequency words: we('ll), of, in, the, a

Interest words: seasons, scrapbook, park, flowers, bees, leaves, robin

Resources: digital camera

Word count: 31

Getting started

- Ask children if they can name any of the seasons and the months of the year. Ask them what happens in each season.

- Look at the front cover together. Read the title and describe what is happening in the four pictures. Help children to match each picture to a season.

- Read the word *scrapbook*. Notice that it is made up of two words. Model how to sound out and blend to read longer words.

- Read the blurb aloud together, pointing at each word. Ask children what they will find in a park in each season.

Reading and responding

- Read p2 together. Practise reading the phrase "We'll find ..." and add an idea from the picture on p3.